SUMMARY OF JOURNEY INTO HIS PRESENCE

Discovering the Flow of Spirit-Led Prayer

MARCUS TANKARD

Copyright 2024–Harrison House

All rights reserved. This book is protected by the copyright laws of the United States of America. This book may not be copied or reprinted for commercial gain or profit. The use of short quotations or occasional page copying for personal or group study is permitted and encouraged. Permission will be granted upon request. Unless otherwise indicated, all scripture quotations are taken from the *King James Version* of the Bible. Used by permission. All rights reserved.

All emphasis within Scripture quotations is the author's own. Please note that Harrison House's publishing style capitalizes certain pronouns in Scripture that refer to the Father, Son, and Holy Spirit, and may differ from some publishers' styles. Take note that the name satan and related names are not capitalized. We choose not to acknowledge him, even to the point of violating grammatical rules.

Harrison House P.O. Box 310, Shippensburg, PA 17257-0310

This book and all other Harrison House's books are available at Christian bookstores and distributors worldwide.

For Worldwide Distribution.

Reach us on the Internet: www.harrisonhouse.com.

ISBN 13 TP: 9781667508238

ISBN 13 eBook: 9781667508245

CONTENTS

Introduction … v

1. God Is Looking for You … 1
2. Welcome to the Presence of the Lord … 4
3. Adventures with the Holy Spirit … 8
4. Speaking in Tongues … 12
5. Recognize the Spirit of Prayer … 16
6. Ministry of Intercession … 19
7. Prayer Assignments … 23
8. The Lost Art of Consecration … 27
9. Finding the Balance in Prayer … 31

About the Publisher … 35

INTRODUCTION

※

"Journey Into His Presence" is a profound exploration of prayer, its power, and its impact on a believer's life. The author draws from personal experiences and biblical principles to provide a comprehensive guide on developing a robust prayer life. This summary encapsulates the key teachings from each chapter, aiming to help readers deepen their relationship with God through effective, balanced, and faith-filled prayer.

The book addresses common struggles in prayer, the importance of intercession, and the role of consecration. It emphasizes the need for a balanced approach to prayer, rooted in scripture and community. Through practical insights and spiritual wisdom, the author encourages believers to embrace prayer as a dynamic and transformative practice.

Each chapter provides specific instructions and encouragements, whether it's finding balance in prayer, understanding prayer assignments, or

INTRODUCTION

learning the art of consecration. The summary distills these teachings into accessible and actionable points, making it a valuable resource for anyone seeking to enrich their prayer life and draw closer to God.

As you read through this summary, may you be inspired to cultivate a deeper, more intimate relationship with God, experiencing the fullness of His presence and the power of answered prayer.

CHAPTER 1

GOD IS LOOKING FOR YOU

Bible Verse

"Then the Lord God called to Adam and said to him, 'Where are you?'" (Genesis 3:9)

Introduction

In this chapter, the author recounts a profound personal experience, illustrating a moment of divine connection and drawing a parallel to God's pursuit of humanity. Through a narrative about meeting his wife, the author emphasizes God's relentless search for a personal relationship with each of us.

Word of Wisdom

"God is always in your presence, but you are not always in His." Marcus Tankard

Main Theme

God's profound desire for an intimate relationship with us mirrors the author's pursuit of his wife, reflecting God's unending quest for our attention and fellowship.

Key Points

- The author met his wife at a church and felt an instant, profound connection.
- This human pursuit is likened to God's desire for our attention and presence.
- God seeks fellowship with humanity, as illustrated in Genesis with Adam and Eve.
- Prayer is a powerful tool for connecting with God and giving Him our full attention.
- God desires worshippers who engage with Him in spirit and truth.
- Intercessors play a crucial role in inviting God's intervention in the world.

Key Themes

- **Divine Pursuit:** The author's experience of meeting his wife serves as a metaphor for how God pursues us. Just as the author felt compelled to know his future wife, God continually seeks a relationship with us.
- **Prayer as Connection:** Prayer is highlighted as the primary means through which we can respond to God's pursuit. It

involves giving God our full attention and receiving His presence.
- **God's Desire for Worship:** True worship requires our complete presence and focus on God, rather than on ourselves or our needs. This type of worship is pure and honors God for who He is.
- **Role of Intercessors:** Intercessors are essential for bringing God's influence into the world. They stand in the gap, praying for nations, families, and individuals, aligning with God's heart and purposes.
- **Supernatural Partnership:** Prayer is more than a discipline; it is a supernatural partnership with God. Through prayer, believers participate in God's power to effect change in the world.

Conclusion

The chapter calls readers to recognize God's persistent search for a relationship with them. By prioritizing prayer and worship, believers can respond to God's call, aligning their lives with His will and experiencing the profound connection He desires. The author encourages a life of intentional prayer and worship, ensuring that God never has to search for our attention.

The overarching message is clear: God is looking for us, and our response should be to seek Him with the same fervor, making prayer and worship central to our lives.

CHAPTER 2

WELCOME TO THE PRESENCE OF THE LORD

Bible Verse

"In my Father's house are many mansions: if it were not so, I would have told you. I go to prepare a place for you."
(John 14:2 KJV)

Introduction

This chapter recounts the author's journey of discovering the omnipresence of God, sparked by a life-changing statement at a worship seminar. It emphasizes that God's presence is always accessible and that Jesus' sacrifice has made this intimate fellowship possible.

Word of Wisdom

"Prayer is easy because Jesus has made it easy." Marcus Tankard

SUMMARY OF JOURNEY INTO HIS PRESENCE

Main Theme

The omnipresence of God is always accessible, and through Jesus, believers are invited to live in continuous fellowship with Him.

Key Points

- A worship seminar statement transformed the author's understanding of God's presence.
- God's presence is always available, even before we start our day.
- Jesus has prepared a space for us to experience God's presence.
- Prayer is a direct invitation into God's presence, made possible by Jesus.
- Believers have unique access to God's presence and power.
- Prayer is not just a right but a responsibility for Christians.

Key Themes

- **Continuous Presence of God:** The realization that God's presence is always available, even before getting out of bed, revolutionized the author's spiritual journey. This accessibility fosters a deeper, more intimate relationship with God.
- **Jesus' Sacrifice and Our Access:** Jesus' death and resurrection created a direct

path for believers to enter God's presence without fear or hesitation. This sacrifice signifies the immense value and availability of God's presence to us.

- **Value of Manifested Presence:** The presence of God is our most valuable asset because of the price Jesus paid. Enjoying this presence honors His sacrifice and allows us to live empowered lives.
- **Transformation through New Creation:** Accepting Jesus changes our existence, making us new creations with the ability to fellowship with God as if we had never sinned. This new identity includes spiritual faculties to engage with God deeply.
- **Freedom in Prayer:** Jesus provides believers with the freedom to express themselves in prayer without fear of judgment. This freedom allows for a genuine, heartfelt connection with God, free from condemnation or embarrassment.

Conclusion

The chapter encourages readers to embrace the ever-present accessibility of God through prayer and worship. By recognizing Jesus' sacrifice and the value of God's presence, believers can confidently approach God, knowing they belong in His presence. This intimate fellowship transforms lives, empowering believers to live in constant communion with God.

SUMMARY OF JOURNEY INTO HIS PRESENCE

The overall message is clear: God's presence is always available, and Jesus has made it easy for us to access it through prayer and worship. Embrace this truth and live a life of continuous fellowship with Him.

CHAPTER 3

ADVENTURES WITH THE HOLY SPIRIT

Bible Verse
"Praying always with all prayer and supplication in the Spirit, being watchful to this end with all perseverance and supplication for all the saints." (Ephesians 6:18)

Introduction

This chapter explores the dynamic and powerful relationship between believers and the Holy Spirit, emphasizing the importance of praying in the Spirit. It highlights the necessity of using the armor of God effectively in prayer and the supernatural guidance available through the Holy Spirit.

Word of Wisdom

"Praying in the Spirit is more than praying in tongues; it is praying under the leadership of the Spirit." Marcus Tankard

SUMMARY OF JOURNEY INTO HIS PRESENCE

Main Theme

The Holy Spirit guides believers in prayer, enabling them to use the armor of God effectively and to pray according to God's will, bringing about powerful results.

Key Points

- The armor of God is meant to be used in prayer, as emphasized in Ephesians 6:18.
- Believers are called to a life of constant prayer, engaging with God continuously.
- Praying in the Spirit involves more than speaking in tongues; it includes being led by the Holy Spirit.
- The Holy Spirit provides direction and inspiration in prayer, going beyond personal agendas.
- Prayer lists should not limit the leading of the Spirit; flexibility in prayer is crucial.
- The Holy Spirit uses believers as God's mouthpiece, declaring His will on earth.

Key Themes

- **Purpose of the Armor of God:** The armor of God is essential for spiritual warfare, and its purpose is fulfilled in the context of prayer. Using the armor in prayer helps believers stand firm against the devil's schemes.

- **Constant Prayer:** Believers are encouraged to practice the presence of God by maintaining a continual dialogue with Him. This constant prayer life strengthens their relationship with God and enhances their spiritual awareness.
- **Praying in the Spirit:** Praying in the Spirit means being led by the Holy Spirit in all forms of prayer, not just praying in tongues. It involves yielding to the Spirit's guidance and praying according to God's will.
- **Flexibility in Prayer:** While prayer lists can be useful, they should not restrict the Holy Spirit's leading. Being open to the Spirit's direction allows for more effective and inspired prayer.
- **Supernatural Partnership:** Prayer is a supernatural partnership with the Holy Spirit. As believers pray, the Holy Spirit reveals God's will, provides direction, and empowers their prayers to bring about divine results.

Conclusion

The chapter calls believers to embrace a dynamic and adventurous prayer life guided by the Holy Spirit. By putting on the armor of God and praying in the Spirit, believers can engage in powerful and effective prayer that aligns with God's will. This partnership with the Holy Spirit transforms prayer into an exciting and impactful journey, leading to profound spiritual growth and divine intervention.

SUMMARY OF JOURNEY INTO HIS PRESENCE

The overarching message is that believers are equipped for spiritual warfare through prayer in the Spirit, and by following the Holy Spirit's guidance, they can experience the full power and presence of God in their lives.

CHAPTER 4

SPEAKING IN TONGUES

Bible Verse

"For he who speaks in a tongue does not speak to men but to God, for no one understands him; however, in the spirit he speaks mysteries." (1 Corinthians 14:2)

Introduction

This chapter delves into the significance of speaking in tongues, a unique and powerful gift of the Holy Spirit reserved for the church age. It explores the supernatural benefits and practical applications of this spiritual practice, emphasizing its role in personal edification and effective prayer.

Word of Wisdom

"Speaking in tongues is a supernatural experience in prayer where an indi-

vidual can pray without being limited by intellect." Marcus Tankard

Main Theme

Speaking in tongues is a divine gift that allows believers to pray beyond their understanding, tapping into the perfect will of God and accessing supernatural benefits for personal and communal growth.

Key Points

- Speaking in tongues is unique to the church age and was not practiced in the Old Testament.
- It allows believers to pray in a supernatural language inspired by the Holy Spirit.
- The experience of speaking in tongues begins with being filled with the Holy Spirit.
- Tongues provide a way to pray perfectly according to God's will.
- This practice is not just ornamental but is essential for spiritual growth and effective prayer.
- Speaking in tongues is available to all believers who are filled with the Holy Spirit.

Key Themes

- **Supernatural Language:** Speaking in tongues is a language provided by the Holy Spirit, transcending human intellect and allowing believers to pray according to God's perfect will.
- **Filled with the Spirit:** The prerequisite to speaking in tongues is being filled with the Holy Spirit, which can be received through prayer or the laying on of hands.
- **Praying for the Unknown:** The Holy Spirit assists believers in prayer by providing utterance for situations beyond their understanding, ensuring prayers align with God's will.
- **Mysteries and Secrets:** Speaking in tongues allows believers to pray out hidden truths and secrets, bringing clarity and guidance for their lives.
- **Self-Improvement:** Praying in tongues builds up the believer, strengthening their spirit and preparing them for the fulfillment of God's plans and promises.

Conclusion

Speaking in tongues is a powerful and essential practice for believers, providing a direct line to God's will and enabling them to pray effectively and grow spiritually. By embracing this gift, believers can experience deeper communion with God and greater alignment with His purposes.

Through speaking in tongues, believers unlock a realm of supernatural prayer that transforms their

SUMMARY OF JOURNEY INTO HIS PRESENCE

lives and brings divine intervention into their circumstances. This practice not only enriches personal spiritual growth but also equips believers to impact their world through prayer.

CHAPTER 5

RECOGNIZE THE SPIRIT OF PRAYER

Bible Verse

"And I will pour on the house of David and on the inhabitants of Jerusalem the Spirit of grace and supplication; then they will look on Me whom they pierced." (Zechariah 12:10)

Introduction

This chapter explores the necessity of recognizing the Holy Spirit's prompts to pray, emphasizing the importance of being available and attentive to His cues. By understanding how the Spirit leads us into prayer, believers can deepen their prayer lives and partner with God more effectively.

Word of Wisdom

"If you want to be used of God in a greater way in prayer, you have to raise

SUMMARY OF JOURNEY INTO HIS PRESENCE

your awareness of His movement in prayer." Marcus Tankard

Main Theme

Recognizing and responding to the Holy Spirit's invitations to pray is essential for believers to effectively partner with God and advance His plans through prayer.

Key Points

- The Holy Spirit constantly seeks partners in prayer.

- Being available to God in prayer is crucial for recognizing His cues.

- Desire to pray often signals the Spirit's leading.

- Restlessness, especially at night, can be a prompt for prayer.

- Prophetic revelations and burdens are invitations to intercede.

- Random thoughts and questions about the future are often cues to pray.

Key Themes

- **Desire to Pray:** A spontaneous urge to pray is a clear sign from the Holy Spirit. Responding to this desire can lead to deeper communion with God and more specific prayer directions.

- **Restlessness:** Nighttime awakenings or general unease can be the Spirit's way of drawing us into urgent prayer. Instead of distracting ourselves, we should engage in prayer to find peace and direction.
- **Prophetic Revelation:** When God reveals something to us, it often comes with a prayer assignment. These revelations should prompt us to pray for individuals, situations, or future events.
- **A Burden:** Feeling a sudden heaviness or burden can indicate that we need to intercede for someone or something. Praying until this burden lifts ensures that we have effectively partnered with the Holy Spirit.
- **Random Thoughts and Questions:** Unexplained thoughts about people or future-related questions can be cues to pray. These prompts should lead us to seek God's guidance and intervention in prayer.

Conclusion

Recognizing the Spirit of prayer involves being sensitive to the Holy Spirit's subtle prompts and making prayer a priority amidst life's demands. By understanding and responding to these cues, believers can effectively partner with God, ensuring that His plans are prayed out and fulfilled.

Through heightened awareness and responsiveness to the Holy Spirit, believers can experience deeper, more impactful prayer lives. This partnership not only enriches personal spiritual growth but also brings God's will into reality on earth.

CHAPTER 6

MINISTRY OF INTERCESSION

Bible Verse

"Therefore I exhort first of all that supplications, prayers, intercessions, and giving of thanks be made for all men." (1 Timothy 2:1)

Introduction

This chapter clarifies the concept of intercession, distinguishing it from general prayer. It explains intercessory prayer as a mediator's role, emphasizing its importance and providing practical guidance for believers to engage effectively in this ministry.

Word of Wisdom

"Intercession is bigger than prayer. It is the act whereby reconciliation is brought to a person who is disconnected from God." Marcus Tankard

Main Theme

Intercession is the act of mediating between God and humanity, primarily for the purpose of reconciliation. Believers are called to join in Christ's intercessory ministry, praying for others and bridging the gap between God and those in need.

Key Points

- Intercession is the act of mediation, not just prayer.
- Jesus' sacrifice is the ultimate act of intercession.
- Believers are co-laborers in Christ's intercessory ministry.
- God actively seeks intercessors to stand in the gap.
- Intercessors make themselves available to pray out God's plans.
- Prophets and intercessors have distinct roles but share the foundation of prayer.

Key Themes

- **Intercession and Jesus' Sacrifice:**
  Intercession involves mediating between God and humanity, exemplified by Jesus' ultimate sacrifice. His death, burial, and resurrection serve as the eternal bridge for reconciliation.
- **Role of Believers in Intercession:**
  Christians are invited to partake in Christ's

ministry by praying for the lost and preaching the word of reconciliation. This shared ministry highlights our role as ambassadors for Christ, representing His love and message to the world.
- **God's Call for Intercessors:** God actively seeks individuals to stand in the gap for others through prayer. Availability and sensitivity to God's heart are essential for effective intercessory prayer, allowing believers to receive and act on prayer assignments from God.
- **Distinguishing Intercession from Supplication:** Intercession focuses on mediating for those facing judgment or separation from God, while supplication involves passionate entreaty for fellow believers. Both are vital aspects of a comprehensive prayer ministry.
- **Prophets and Intercessors:** While all believers are called to intercede, prophets have a unique role that includes seeing and declaring God's messages. However, intercessors should avoid assuming prophetic responsibilities without clear calling and guidance.

Conclusion

Intercession is a vital ministry that extends beyond prayer, involving mediation and reconciliation between God and humanity. By understanding and embracing this role, believers can effectively partner with Christ in His intercessory work. This partnership requires dedication, availability, and sensitivity to God's leading, ensuring that intercessory prayer is both powerful and transformative.

Intercession invites believers to deeply engage with God's heart and participate in His redemptive work. By answering this call, believers can bridge the gap for others, bringing God's grace and reconciliation to those in need.

CHAPTER 7

PRAYER ASSIGNMENTS

Bible Verse

"I urge, then, first of all, that petitions, prayers, intercession and thanksgiving be made for all people." (1 Timothy 2:1)

Introduction

This chapter explores the concept of prayer assignments, emphasizing their importance in partnering with God to fulfill His plans on earth. It details the three primary prayer assignments given to every believer and explains how to recognize and respond to these divine directives.

Word of Wisdom

"God is looking for believers who will commit to pray. He's looking for someone who will enter the prayer place and co-

labor with Him in His plan." Marcus Tankard

Main Theme

Prayer assignments are divine tasks given to believers to pray for specific purposes, such as God's plan for their lives, all people, and the harvest. Recognizing and faithfully responding to these assignments aligns believers with God's heart and plans.

Key Points

• Prayer assignments involve partnering with God to fulfill His plans.

• Believers are called to pray for God's plan for their lives.

• Praying for all people, especially leaders, is crucial.

• The harvest needs focused, strategic prayer.

• Recognizing prayer assignments requires spiritual sensitivity.

• Faithfulness in prayer leads to greater anointing and clarity.

SUMMARY OF JOURNEY INTO HIS PRESENCE

Key Themes

- **God's Plan for Your Life:** Praying out God's plan for your life is essential and personal. It involves continually seeking God for guidance and aligning your actions with His will, ensuring you are in the right place at the right time with the right people.
- **Praying for All People:** The call to pray for all people focuses on interceding for leaders, as their decisions impact entire communities. Praying for leaders ensures that peace, godliness, and holiness prevail, aligning with God's desire for all to be saved.
- **The Harvest:** Praying for the harvest involves asking God to send skilled laborers to reach those who need to hear the gospel. This type of prayer ensures that the right people are in the right place to sow and water the seeds of God's word effectively.
- **Discerning Prayer Assignments:** Recognizing prayer assignments starts with understanding the three primary ones outlined in the Bible. As believers commit to these foundational assignments, they become more sensitive to additional, specific directives from God.
- **Anointed to Pray:** Believers are anointed by the Spirit to fulfill their prayer assignments. This anointing provides the revelation, utterance, and leading needed to pray effectively, ensuring that God's

plans are prayed out and accomplished on earth.

Conclusion

Prayer assignments are a vital part of a believer's spiritual journey, enabling them to partner with God in fulfilling His plans. By committing to pray for God's plan for their lives, all people, and the harvest, believers align themselves with God's heart and purposes. Faithfulness in these assignments brings greater anointing, clarity, and effectiveness in prayer.

Embracing these prayer assignments and being sensitive to God's leading will empower believers to make a significant impact through their prayers, ensuring that God's will is done on earth as it is in heaven.

CHAPTER 8

THE LOST ART OF CONSECRATION

Bible Verse

"Consecrate yourselves, for tomorrow the Lord will do amazing things among you." (Joshua 3:5 NIV)

Introduction

This chapter delves into the concept of consecration, which means separating oneself from anything unclean and dedicating oneself to what is spiritual. It highlights the importance of consecration in experiencing God's amazing blessings and aligning oneself with His presence and plans.

Word of Wisdom

"Consecration is not a performance-based activity destined to earn God's attention and favor. Consecration is how you move into the fullness of God's favor

and presence for your life." Marcus Tankard

Main Theme

Consecration involves separating from what is profane and dedicating oneself to God. It is essential for experiencing the fullness of God's favor and presence, and it requires intentional acts of prayer, fasting, and giving.

Key Points

• Consecration means separating from the unclean and dedicating to the spiritual.

• Consecration leads to experiencing amazing blessings from God.

• Prayer, fasting, and giving are key expressions of consecration.

• Consecration is a continual, intentional process.

• Jesus taught that certain spiritual breakthroughs require prayer and fasting.

• Consecration should not be seen as earning God's favor but embracing His gifts.

Key Themes

- **The Meaning of Consecration:**
  Consecration is about separating oneself from anything unclean and dedicating

oneself to God. It involves a deliberate focus on what is spiritual and godly, as illustrated in Joshua 3:5, where consecration precedes experiencing God's wonders.

- **The Importance of Prayer:** Consecration through prayer allows believers to delve deeper into God's presence and wisdom. By setting aside time for prayer, believers draw nearer to God and access hidden truths and guidance necessary for their lives.
- **The Role of Fasting:** Fasting is abstaining from food to gain spiritual strength and discipline. It helps believers exercise dominion over their flesh, align their minds and emotions with God's will, and prepare themselves for greater spiritual tasks and revelations.
- **The Act of Giving:** Giving sacrificially as part of consecration demonstrates trust in God and opens the heart to receive His revelation. It aligns one's affections with God's plan and expands the capacity to hear and follow His direction.
- **Consecration in Daily Life:** Consecration is an ongoing practice, not a one-time event. It involves regular, intentional acts of prayer, fasting, and giving, which together help believers stay aligned with God's purposes and sensitive to His leading.

Conclusion

Consecration is a vital spiritual discipline that

aligns believers with God's presence and plans. Through prayer, fasting, and giving, believers draw nearer to God, receive His wisdom, and prepare themselves for His purposes. Embracing the art of consecration leads to a deeper, more fruitful relationship with God and the unfolding of His amazing blessings in one's life.

CHAPTER 9

FINDING THE BALANCE IN PRAYER

Bible Verse
"And without faith it is impossible to please Him, for whoever would draw near to God must believe that He exists and that He rewards those who seek Him."
(Hebrews 11:6 ESV)

Introduction

In this chapter, the author explores the importance of maintaining biblical boundaries in prayer. Effective prayer disrupts the devil's dominion, but it requires habits and discipline. The chapter provides practical insights and habits to help believers stay balanced and effective in their prayer lives.

Word of Wisdom

"A balanced prayer life is a fruitful one. Jesus ordained you to bear fruit in

prayer—the fruit is answered prayer."
Marcus Tankard

Main Theme

Achieving balance in prayer is crucial for effectiveness. By adhering to biblical principles and integrating good habits, believers can ensure their prayers are powerful and aligned with God's will.

Key Points

• Stay connected to the local church for spiritual impartations and balance.

• Seek prayer mentors to guide and challenge your prayer life.

• Maintain humility to avoid pride and error in prayer.

• Study the Word more than you pray to stay grounded.

• Avoid an overemphasis on conspiracy theories to stay focused on truth.

• Recognize and help "flaky" Christians with compassion and guidance.

Key Themes

- **Stay Connected to the Local Church:**
  Regular church attendance and participation are essential for balanced

prayer life. The local church provides spiritual impartations and keeps believers grounded in doctrine, ensuring they don't stray in their prayer practices.
- **Seek Prayer Mentors:** Having mentors who are grounded in the Word and skilled in prayer helps maintain sobriety and effectiveness in prayer. Mentors can offer guidance, correct misinterpretations, and encourage growth in prayer.
- **Maintain Humility:** Pride can derail a believer's prayer life. Staying humble ensures that one remains teachable and receptive to God's guidance, fostering a healthier, more effective prayer journey.
- **Prioritize the Word:** The Word of God is essential for effective prayer. Studying the Bible regularly provides the necessary "spirit fuel" for prayer, ensuring that prayers are aligned with God's truth and will.
- **Avoid Conspiracy Theories:** Overindulgence in conspiracy theories fosters suspicion and fear, which are counterproductive to a faith-filled prayer life. Staying focused on the truth of God's Word prevents deception and maintains the purity of prayer intentions.

Conclusion

A balanced prayer life, rooted in the Word of God and supported by the local church and prayer mentors, is essential for effectiveness. Avoiding pride, conspiracy theories, and flaky behaviors ensures that prayers remain powerful and aligned with God's will. By fostering these habits, believers can experience the fruitfulness and joy of answered prayers, deepening their journey into God's presence.

Harrison House is a Spirit-filled, Word of Faith Christian publisher dedicated to spreading the message of faith, hope, and love through our wide range of inspiring publications. Committed to the messages that highlight the power of the Word and Spirit, we provide books, devotionals, and study guides that empower believers to live victorious, faith-filled lives.

Our resources are designed to help readers grow spiritually, strengthen their faith, and experience the transformative power of God's Word. Harrison House is passionate about equipping Christians with the tools they need to fulfill their divine purpose and impact the world for Christ.

Milton Keynes UK
Ingram Content Group UK Ltd.
UKHW022032131124
451149UK00015B/1412